SPORTS BOOK

Copyright © 2024 by Mary Widkins. All Rights Reserved.

No part of this publication or the information in it may be quoted from or reproduced in any form by means such as printing, scanning, photocopying or otherwise without prior written permission of the copyright holder. Disclaimer and Terms of Use: Effort has been made to ensure that the information in this book is accurate and complete. However, the author and the publisher do not warrant the accuracy of the information, text and graphics contained within the book due to the rapidly changing nature of science, research, known and unknown facts and the Internet. The author and the publisher do not hold any responsibility for errors, omissions or contrary interpretations of the subject matter herein.

INTRODUCTION

Welcome to the thrilling world of the Sports Trivia Book, your ultimate guide to testing your knowledge across a wide array of sports. This book is designed not only for the avid sports enthusiast but also for those who are just beginning to dip their toes into the vast ocean of sports history, achievements, controversies, and cultural exchanges. This format is advantageous for several reasons:

Accessibility: Whether you're a seasoned trivia veteran or a curious newcomer, the multiple-choice format makes it easy for anyone to participate. It encourages learning and exploration, turning every question into an opportunity for discovery.

Variety: With questions covering a diverse range of sports, including soccer, basketball, the Olympics, baseball, and more, this book offers a comprehensive look at the world of sports. The variety ensures something for everyone, regardless of your favorite sport or league.

Engagement: The multiple-choice format keeps you engaged and on your toes. It challenges you to recall information, deduce answers, and learn new facts about sports you thought you knew well.

Community: This book is a fantastic tool for bringing together friends, family, and sports fans. It's perfect for game nights, sports-themed parties, or to spark lively discussions and friendly debates about the most unforgettable moments in sports history.

Educational Value: Beyond the entertainment, the Sports Trivia Book is a valuable educational resource. It delves into history geography, and even touches on important social issues within the realm of sports. Each question is an opportunity to expand your knowledge and gain a deeper appreciation for the world of sports.

Grab your pen, gather your friends, and prepare to challenge your mind and ignite your passion for sports. Welcome to the Sports Trivia Book, where every question is a chance to relive the glory, the drama, and the unbreakable spirit of athletes and teams from around the globe. Let the games begin!

TABLE OF CONTENTS

Basketball..5

Baseball..18

American Football.................................31

Ice Hockey..44

Combat Sports (Boxing & MMA)..........57

College Sports..70

Olympics..84

Soccer..97

Answers...111

★★★★★

SHARE YOUR THOUGHTS!

Dear Reader,

As the author, I find your feedback invaluable. Your insights and opinions enhance my understanding of this book's impact and significantly influence my future work! Please consider leaving an honest review because your feedback guides other readers and helps us grow.

How to Leave a Review

Scan the QR code, which will take you to the review page.

Your voice matters. Lend it to the conversation and help shape future reads!

Thank you.

Basketball

1. Who was the first player to shatter a backboard during an NBA game?
a. Michael Jordan
b. Wilt Chamberlain
c. Shaquille O'Neal
d. Charles Barkley

2. Which player was known as the first superstar of the NBA?
a. Bob Cousy
b. George Mikan
c. Bill Russell
d. Jerry West

3. Who was the first African American to play in an NBA game?
a. Chuck Cooper
b. Earl Lloyd
c. Nat "Sweetwater" Clifton
d. Bill Russell

4. Who is considered the inventor of the jump shot?
a. Joe Fulks
b. Kenny Sailors
c. Paul Arizin
d. George Yardley

5. Which player was the first to achieve a quadruple-double in an NBA game?
a. Hakeem Olajuwon
b. David Robinson
c. Nate Thurmond

d. Alvin Robertson

6. Who was the first player to score 100 points in a single NBA game?
a. Kobe Bryant
b. Michael Jordan
c. Wilt Chamberlain
d. LeBron James

7. Who was the first woman to be drafted by an NBA team?
a. Cheryl Miller
b. Ann Meyers
c. Teresa Weatherspoon
d. Lisa Leslie

8. Which coach is credited with inventing the fast break?
a. Red Auerbach
b. John Wooden
c. Phil Jackson
d. Pat Riley

9. Who was the first NBA player officially recognized as the Most Valuable Player (MVP)?
a. Bob Pettit
b. Bill Russell
c. Oscar Robertson
d. Wilt Chamberlain

10. Which player broke the color barrier by becoming the first African American to sign an

NBA contract?
a. Chuck Cooper
b. Earl Lloyd
c. Nat "Sweetwater" Clifton
d. Bill Russell

11. Who was the first player to introduce the "point forward" concept in the NBA?
a. Magic Johnson
b. Scottie Pippen
c. John Havlicek
d. Paul Pressey

12. Who was the first player in NBA history to be elected league MVP by a unanimous vote?
a. Michael Jordan
b. LeBron James
c. Stephen Curry
d. Shaquille O'Neal

13. In which year did Michael Jordan hit "The Shot" over Craig Ehlo in the playoffs?
a. 1989
b. 1991
c. 1993
d. 1995

14. Who made the game-winning shot in Game 6 of the 1998 NBA Finals?
a. Karl Malone
b. Michael Jordan
c. Scottie Pippen

d. John Stockton

15. Which team completed the largest comeback in NBA playoffs history?
a. Boston Celtics
b. Los Angeles Clippers
c. Golden State Warriors
d. Cleveland Cavaliers

16. Who hit the buzzer-beater three-pointer to win the game for the Toronto Raptors in Game 7 of the 2019 Eastern Conference Semifinals?
a. Kawhi Leonard
b. Kyle Lowry
c. Pascal Siakam
d. Fred VanVleet

17. What was notable about the 1984 NBA Finals Game 7 between the Boston Celtics and the Los Angeles Lakers?
a. Highest-scoring game in Finals history
b. First Finals game was decided in triple overtime
c. Celtics' Cedric Maxwell urged teammates to "hop on my back"
d. Magic Johnson played all five positions

18. Which team broke the record for the most wins in a regular season?
a. 1995-96 Chicago Bulls
b. 2015-16 Golden State Warriors
c. 1985-86 Boston Celtics
d. 2000-01 Los Angeles Lakers

19. In the "Flu Game," Michael Jordan scored 38 points against which team in the 1997 NBA Finals?
a. Portland Trail Blazers
b. Seattle SuperSonics
c. Utah Jazz
d. Los Angeles Lakers

20. Who made a series-winning shot against the Houston Rockets in the first round of the 2014 NBA playoffs?
a. Damian Lillard
b. Russell Westbrook
c. James Harden
d. Kevin Durant

21. Which player's iconic leap from the free-throw line won the 1988 NBA Slam Dunk Contest?
a. Dominique Wilkins
b. Michael Jordan
c. Vince Carter
d. Julius Erving

22. The "Malice at the Palace" brawl occurred during a game between the Indiana Pacers and which other team?
a. Detroit Pistons
b. Chicago Bulls
c. New York Knicks
d. Miami Heat

23. Which NBA Finals saw Ray Allen hit a crucial game-tying three-pointer in Game 6, leading to an overtime win and eventual championship for the Miami Heat?
a. 2012
b. 2013
c. 2014
d. 2015

24. Who holds the record for the most points scored in a single NBA season?
a. Michael Jordan
b. LeBron James
c. Kobe Bryant
d. Wilt Chamberlain

25. What is the highest number of rebounds recorded in a single NBA game?
a. 55
b. 50
c. 49
d. 55

26. Who has the most career assists in NBA history?
a. Magic Johnson
b. Steve Nash
c. John Stockton
d. Jason Kidd

27. Which player achieved the fastest triple-double in NBA history?
a. Russell Westbrook
b. Nikola Jokić
c. LeBron James
d. Jim Tucker

28. Who is the youngest player to score 10,000 points in the NBA?
a. Kobe Bryant
b. LeBron James
c. Kevin Durant
d. Michael Jordan

29. Which player has won the most NBA MVP awards?
a. Michael Jordan
b. LeBron James
c. Kareem Abdul-Jabbar
d. Bill Russell

30. Who has the most career steals in NBA history?
a. Michael Jordan
b. Gary Payton
c. John Stockton
d. Jason Kidd

31. What is the record for most three-pointers made in a single NBA game?
a. 12
b. 13
c. 14

d. 15

32. Who holds the NBA record for most points in a playoff game?
a. LeBron James
b. Michael Jordan
c. Kobe Bryant
d. Elgin Baylor

33. What is the most number of blocks recorded in a single NBA game?
a. 11
b. 12
c. 15
d. 17

34. Who achieved the most consecutive double-doubles in NBA history?
a. Wilt Chamberlain
b. Bill Russell
c. Karl Malone
d. Kevin Love

35. Who has the most career rebounds in NBA history?
a. Bill Russell
b. Wilt Chamberlain
c. Kareem Abdul-Jabbar
d. Tim Duncan

36. Which player has the most career triple-doubles in the NBA?
a. Magic Johnson
b. Russell Westbrook
c. LeBron James
d. Jason Kidd

37. Which country won the first-ever basketball gold medal at the Olympics?
a. United States
b. Soviet Union
c. Canada
d. Argentina

38. Who was the first European player to win the NBA MVP Award?
a. Dirk Nowitzki
b. Pau Gasol
c. Giannis Antetokounmpo
d. Tony Parker

39. Which country hosted the first Basketball World Cup outside of the Americas in 1970?
a. Yugoslavia
b. Spain
c. Italy
d. France

40. Who is the first Asian player to be drafted as the number one overall pick in the NBA Draft?
a. Yao Ming
b. Yi Jianlian

c. Wataru Misaka
d. Hedo Turkoglu

41. What year was basketball first included as an Olympic sport?
a. 1936
b. 1948
c. 1952
d. 1960

42. Which African country was the first to win a game at the Basketball World Cup?
a. Nigeria
b. Angola
c. Senegal
d. Egypt

43. Who was the first non-American to win the NBA Rookie of the Year Award?
a. Patrick Ewing
b. Dirk Nowitzki
c. Pau Gasol
d. Steve Nash

44. Which city hosted the first official World Basketball Championship, the FIBA Basketball World Cup?
a. Buenos Aires, Argentina
b. Madrid, Spain
c. Athens, Greece
d. Istanbul, Turkey

45. Who was the first African-born player to win an NBA championship?
a. Manute Bol
b. Dikembe Mutombo
c. Hakeem Olajuwon
d. Joel Embiid

46. Which country's national team is known as the "Tall Blacks"?
a. Australia
b. New Zealand
c. Canada
d. South Africa

47. What is the name of the prestigious international basketball competition held in Asia?
a. Asian Games
b. FIBA Asia Cup
c. Asian Basketball Championship
d. ASEAN Basketball League

48. Who was the first Brazilian player inducted into the Naismith Memorial Basketball Hall of Fame?
a. Nene Hilario
b. Oscar Schmidt
c. Anderson Varejão
d. Leandro Barbosa

49. Which European country won its first Olympic basketball gold medal in 1980?
a. Soviet Union
b. Yugoslavia
c. Spain
d. Italy

50. Who is the highest-scoring Asian player in NBA history?
a. Yao Ming
b. Jeremy Lin
c. Yuta Watanabe
d. Rui Hachimura

Baseball

51. In what year was the National League of Professional Baseball Clubs originally founded, now known simply as the National League (NL)?
a. 1876
b. 1890
c. 1901
d. 1912

52. Who is credited with being the "Father of Baseball" for standardizing the game's rules?
a. Abner Doubleday
b. Alexander Cartwright
c. Babe Ruth
d. Henry Chadwick

53. The first recorded baseball game under Cartwright's rules was played in which location?
a. Hoboken, New Jersey
b. Cooperstown, New York
c. Boston, Massachusetts
d. Chicago, Illinois

54. Which team won the first modern World Series in 1903?
a. New York Yankees
b. Boston Red Sox
c. Chicago Cubs
d. Pittsburgh Pirates

55. The Cincinnati Red Stockings are recognized as the first entirely professional baseball team. In what year did they become professional?
a. 1869
b. 1875
c. 1882
d. 1890

56. What significant baseball event occurred in 1869?
a. The first professional baseball team was formed
b. The first recorded game using modern rules was played
c. The National League was founded
d. The first baseball stadium was built

57. Who was the first president of the National League when it was founded in 1876?
a. William Hulbert
b. Albert Spalding
c. Harry Wright
d. Morgan Bulkeley

58. The Knickerbocker Baseball Club, one of the earliest baseball teams, was founded in which city?
a. New York City
b. Philadelphia
c. Boston
d. Baltimore

59. What year was the American League (AL) established as a major league?
a. 1894
b. 1901
c. 1903
d. 1912

60. Which invention in 1845 significantly impacted how baseball was played?
a. The baseball glove
b. The catcher's mask
c. The baseball bat
d. The baseball diamond

61. Which two teams played the first official game of baseball?
a. New York Nine and Knickerbocker Club
b. Boston Red Sox and New York Yankees
c. Cincinnati Red Stockings and Chicago White Stockings
d. Philadelphia Athletics and Boston Red Stockings

62. Who is known for publishing the first set of baseball rules that closely resemble the game today?
a. Abner Doubleday
b. Alexander Cartwright
c. Babe Ruth
d. Henry Chadwick

63. Who was the first player in Major League Baseball to have his number retired?
a. Babe Ruth
b. Jackie Robinson
c. Lou Gehrig
d. Ty Cobb

64. Which player broke Babe Ruth's all-time home run record in 1974?
a. Hank Aaron
b. Barry Bonds
c. Willie Mays
d. Mickey Mantle

65. What nickname was given to the 1927 New York Yankees team, considered one of the greatest in baseball history?
a. The Bronx Bombers
b. Murderers' Row
c. The Iron Horsemen
d. The Big Red Machine

66. Which player holds the record for most hits in a single season?
a. Pete Rose
b. Ty Cobb
c. Ichiro Suzuki
d. Ted Williams

67. Who was the first African American player in the modern era to play Major League Baseball?
a. Satchel Paige

b. Jackie Robinson
c. Larry Doby
d. Hank Aaron

68. What team did Babe Ruth play for before joining the New York Yankees?
a. Boston Red Sox
b. Chicago White Sox
c. Brooklyn Dodgers
d. Pittsburgh Pirates

69. Which player has won the most World Series titles as a player?
a. Yogi Berra
b. Babe Ruth
c. Joe DiMaggio
d. Mickey Mantle

70. Who is the only player in MLB history to hit four home runs in a single game twice?
a. Lou Gehrig
b. Sammy Sosa
c. Mike Schmidt
d. Josh Hamilton

71. Which pitcher holds the record for most career strikeouts?
a. Nolan Ryan
b. Roger Clemens
c. Randy Johnson
d. Sandy Koufax

72. The "Shot Heard 'Round the World" was a famous home run hit by which player?
a. Joe Carter
b. Bill Mazeroski
c. Bobby Thomson
d. Kirk Gibson

73. Who was the first player in MLB history to be named Most Valuable Player (MVP) in both the American and National Leagues?
a. Frank Robinson
b. Barry Bonds
c. Ken Griffey Jr.
d. Alex Rodriguez

74. Which team ended the "Curse of the Bambino" by winning the World Series in 2004?
a. New York Yankees
b. Boston Red Sox
c. Chicago Cubs
d. St. Louis Cardinals

75. Which team won the World Series in 1986 after a famous error by Bill Buckner in Game 6?
a. New York Mets
b. Boston Red Sox
c. Chicago Cubs
d. Los Angeles Dodgers

76. The 2001 World Series featured a dramatic Game 7 walk-off hit. Which team was victorious?
a. Arizona Diamondbacks

b. New York Yankees
c. San Francisco Giants
d. Atlanta Braves

77. Who hit the "Shot Heard 'Round the World" to win the National League pennant leading to the 1951 World Series?
a. Mickey Mantle
b. Willie Mays
c. Bobby Thomson
d. Joe DiMaggio

78. What year did the Chicago Cubs break their 108-year World Series championship drought?
a. 2016
b. 2004
c. 1988
d. 2000

79. Who was the World Series MVP when the Boston Red Sox ended their 86-year championship drought in 2004?
a. David Ortiz
b. Manny Ramirez
c. Curt Schilling
d. Pedro Martinez

80. Which World Series is known for the "Earthquake Series" due to a significant earthquake occurring before Game 3?
a. 1989 World Series
b. 1994 World Series

c. 2002 World Series
d. 2010 World Series

81. What team overcame a 3-1 series deficit to win the World Series 2016?
a. Chicago Cubs
b. Cleveland Indians
c. Kansas City Royals
d. Houston Astros

82. Which team won their first World Series title in 2019?
a. Washington Nationals
b. Houston Astros
c. Los Angeles Dodgers
d. Tampa Bay Rays

83. In which World Series did Reggie Jackson earn the nickname "Mr. October" for his clutch hitting?
a. 1977 World Series
b. 1981 World Series
c. 1973 World Series
d. 1986 World Series

84. Who pitched a perfect game in the World Series, the only one in its history, in 1956?
a. Sandy Koufax
b. Don Larsen
c. Bob Gibson
d. Whitey Ford

85. Which team completed a sweep in the 2007 World Series?
a. Boston Red Sox
b. Chicago White Sox
c. San Francisco Giants
d. New York Yankees

86. The "Miracle Mets" won the World Series in what year?
a. 1969
b. 1973
c. 1986
d. 2000

87. Which team won the World Series in 1995, marking their first championship since moving to Atlanta?
a. Atlanta Braves
b. Minnesota Twins
c. Toronto Blue Jays
d. Cleveland Indians

88. Which MLB team is known for having a live mascot race featuring former U.S. Presidents?
a. Washington Nationals
b. Milwaukee Brewers
c. Philadelphia Phillies
d. Texas Rangers

89. What unique feature was installed in Minute Maid Park, home of the Houston Astros?
a. A hill in center field

b. A swimming pool
c. A retractable roof
d. A train that moves when a home run is hit

90. Who was the first major league player to have his ashes scattered at his team's ballpark?
a. Babe Ruth
b. Lou Gehrig
c. Mickey Mantle
d. Thurman Munson

91. Which ballpark is known for its "Ivy-Covered Walls"?
a. Fenway Park
b. Dodger Stadium
c. Wrigley Field
d. Yankee Stadium

92. In what year did an MLB team wear shorts during a game for the first time?
a. 1976
b. 1982
c. 1990
d. 2003

93. What is the name of the infamous cat that ran onto the field during a critical 1969 New York Mets game, leading to superstitions about their championship win?
a. Felix
b. Shadow
c. Whiskers

d. Black Cat

94. Which player is known for eating fried chicken before games as a good luck charm?
a. Wade Boggs
b. Babe Ruth
c. Derek Jeter
d. Pete Rose

95. The term "Mendoza Line" refers to a batting average of:
a. .200
b. .250
c. .300
d. .350

96. What unique food item is famously thrown onto the field at Detroit Tigers games after a player hits a grand slam?
a. Hot dogs
b. Octopus
c. Apples
d. Oranges

97. Which player set a record by playing all nine positions in a single game?
a. Bert Campaneris
b. Cesar Tovar
c. Scott Sheldon
d. Shane Halter

98. What unusual item did San Francisco Giants fans throw onto the field in 1982 to celebrate a home run?
a. Rubber chickens
b. Beach balls
c. Toy boats
d. Tortillas

99. Who is the only player in MLB history to hit a home run off a pitch that bounced before reaching the plate?
a. Mickey Mantle
b. Babe Ruth
c. Vladimir Guerrero
d. Roberto Clemente

100. Which team's fans are known for performing the "Tomahawk Chop" during games?
a. Atlanta Braves
b. Kansas City Royals
c. Cleveland Indians
d. Chicago Blackhawks

American Football

101. What year was the American Professional Football Association, which would later become the NFL, founded?
a. 1919
b. 1920
c. 1921
d. 1922

102. Which year was the first Super Bowl played?
a. 1960
b. 1965
c. 1967
d. 1970

103. Which team implemented the first use of the "huddle" during games?
a. Chicago Bears
b. Green Bay Packers
c. New York Giants
d. Gallaudet University

104. What year was the forward pass legalized in American football?
a. 1906
b. 1912
c. 1920
d. 1933

105. Who is known as the "Father of American Football" for his role in shaping the early rules of the game?
a. Walter Camp

b. Vince Lombardi
c. Knute Rockne
d. George Halas

106. The "T formation" is credited with modernizing offense in football. Which coach is most associated with popularizing this formation?
a. Curly Lambeau
b. George Halas
c. Tom Landry
d. Bill Walsh

107. What significant change did the NFL make in 1974 to increase scoring?
a. Introducing the two-point conversion
b. Moving the goalposts to the back of the end zone
c. Legalizing the forward pass
d. Reducing the distance for a first down to 9 yards

108. What year was the concept of "Monday Night Football" introduced?
a. 1960
b. 1970
c. 1980
d. 1990

109. Who was the first African American head coach in the modern NFL era?
a. Art Shell
b. Tony Dungy
c. Lovie Smith

d. Fritz Pollard

110. What year did the NFL introduce instant replay reviews?
a. 1986
b. 1992
c. 1999
d. 2004

111. Which team is credited with creating the concept of the "no-huddle" offense in the 1980s?
a. San Francisco 49ers
b. Cincinnati Bengals
c. Buffalo Bills
d. Dallas Cowboys

112. What year was the AFL-NFL merger completed, leading to the creation of the modern NFL?
a. 1966
b. 1970
c. 1976
d. 1982

113. Who was the first player to win Super Bowl MVP honors in back-to-back years?
a. Joe Montana
b. Terry Bradshaw
c. Bart Starr
d. Tom Brady

114. Which player holds the record for the most career touchdowns in Super Bowl history?
a. Jerry Rice
b. Emmitt Smith
c. Franco Harris
d. Rob Gronkowski

115. Who is the only defensive player to win Super Bowl MVP without recording a sack or interception?
a. Harvey Martin
b. Randy White
c. Ray Lewis
d. Malcolm Smith

116. What quarterback led the largest comeback in Super Bowl history?
a. Eli Manning
b. Peyton Manning
c. Tom Brady
d. Joe Montana

117. Which team won three Super Bowls in the 1990s?
a. San Francisco 49ers
b. Dallas Cowboys
c. Pittsburgh Steelers
d. New England Patriots

118. Who was the first wide receiver to win Super Bowl MVP?
a. Lynn Swann

b. Jerry Rice
c. Santonio Holmes
d. Julian Edelman

119. The "Immaculate Reception" is associated with which team's journey to their Super Bowl win?
a. Dallas Cowboys
b. Pittsburgh Steelers
c. Oakland Raiders
d. Miami Dolphins

120. Who performed the iconic "helicopter spin" during a Super Bowl XXXII first down run?
a. Brett Favre
b. John Elway
c. Steve Young
d. Troy Aikman

121. Which player has the most career Super Bowl interceptions?
a. Rod Martin
b. Larry Brown
c. Mel Blount
d. Ronnie Lott

122. What kicker made the game-winning field goal as time expired in Super Bowl XXXVI?
a. Adam Vinatieri
b. Stephen Gostkowski
c. Matt Stover
d. Jason Elam

123. Who was the MVP of the first Super Bowl?
a. Len Dawson
b. Bart Starr
c. Joe Namath
d. Roger Staubach

124. Which head coach has the most Super Bowl wins?
a. Bill Belichick
b. Chuck Noll
c. Vince Lombardi
d. Bill Walsh

125. Who is credited with creating the West Coast Offense?
a. Vince Lombardi
b. Bill Walsh
c. Don Shula
d. Bill Belichick

126. Which coach is known for the invention of the "46 defense"?
a. Buddy Ryan
b. Chuck Noll
c. Tom Landry
d. Bill Parcells

127. Who pioneered the use of the no-huddle offense in the NFL?
a. Marv Levy
b. Sam Wyche

c. Bill Walsh
d. Sean Payton

128. Which coach is known for the innovative "Air Coryell" passing offense?
a. Don Coryell
b. Mike Martz
c. Norv Turner
d. Andy Reid

129. The "Tampa 2" defense is associated with which NFL coach?
a. Tony Dungy
b. Lovie Smith
c. Monte Kiffin
d. Rod Marinelli

130. Who introduced the "Pistol Offense" to the NFL?
a. Chip Kelly
b. Jim Harbaugh
c. Bill Belichick
d. Pete Carroll

131. Which coach won Super Bowls with two different teams, known for his adaptability?
a. Bill Parcells
b. Vince Lombardi
c. Mike Shanahan
d. Tom Coughlin

132. Under which coach did the "Wildcat" offense see a resurgence in the NFL?
a. Tony Sparano
b. Sean McVay
c. Adam Gase
d. Doug Pederson

133. Who is the coach credited with creating the "Legion of Boom" defense?
a. Pete Carroll
b. Bill Belichick
c. Vic Fangio
d. Rex Ryan

134. Which coach's strategy is known for the "K-Gun" offense?
a. Marv Levy
b. Sean Payton
c. Andy Reid
d. Joe Gibbs

135. Who pioneered the "Flex Defense" in the NFL?
a. Tom Landry
b. Chuck Noll
c. Bill Belichick
d. George Allen

136. The innovative "Smashmouth Football" strategy is most associated with which coach?
a. Bill Cowher
b. John Madden

c. Mike Ditka
d. Jeff Fisher

137. Who is known for developing the "Greatest Show on Turf", a high-powered offense in the late 1990s and early 2000s?
a. Dick Vermeil
b. Mike Martz
c. Sean McVay
d. Norv Turner

138. Which NFL team's fans are known as the "12th Man"?
a. Seattle Seahawks
b. Green Bay Packers
c. Pittsburgh Steelers
d. New England Patriots

139. The "Lambeau Leap" is a touchdown celebration associated with which team?
a. Green Bay Packers
b. Dallas Cowboys
c. Chicago Bears
d. Detroit Lions

140. "The Black Hole" is famously associated with which team's fans?
a. Las Vegas Raiders
b. Philadelphia Eagles
c. New Orleans Saints d. Baltimore Ravens

141. What item is traditionally thrown onto the field by Detroit Lions fans during Thanksgiving games?
a. Turkeys
b. Footballs
c. Hats
d. Plastic Turkeys

142. Which team's fans are known for wearing "Cheesehead" hats?
a. Green Bay Packers
b. Kansas City Chiefs
c. Denver Broncos
d. Buffalo Bills

143. Which NFL team is the "Terrible Towel" a fan item associated with?
a. Pittsburgh Steelers
b. Cleveland Browns
c. Cincinnati Bengals
d. Baltimore Ravens

144. "Who Dat?" is a chant associated with fans of which NFL team?
a. New Orleans Saints
b. Atlanta Falcons
c. Carolina Panthers
d. Tampa Bay Buccaneers

145. The "Dawg Pound" is the name of the fan section for which NFL team?
a. Cleveland Browns
b. Philadelphia Eagles
c. Denver Broncos
d. Buffalo Bills

146. Which team's fans are known for tailgating with a dish called "Buffalo Wings"?
a. Buffalo Bills
b. Miami Dolphins
c. New York Jets
d. New England Patriots

147. The tradition of performing the "Tomahawk Chop" chant originated with fans of which team?
a. Atlanta Braves
b. Kansas City Chiefs
c. Florida State Seminoles
d. Washington Football Team

148. Which NFL team's fans are known for the "Gjallarhorn" tradition?
a. Minnesota Vikings
b. Seattle Seahawks
c. Green Bay Packers
d. Chicago Bears

149. "Bills Mafia" is a fan movement associated with which NFL team?
a. Buffalo Bills
b. Miami Dolphins

c. New York Jets
d. New England Patriots

150. The tradition of wearing "Fireman Hats" and leading chants was popularized by a fan of which team?
a. New York Jets
b. Dallas Cowboys
c. San Francisco 49ers
d. Philadelphia Eagles

Ice Hockey

151. Who was the first player to score 50 goals in a single NHL season?
a.   Gordie Howe
b.   Maurice Richard
c.   Wayne Gretzky
d.   Bobby Hull

152. Which player holds the record for most points in a single season?
a.   Mario Lemieux
b.   Wayne Gretzky
c.   Sidney Crosby
d.   Jaromir Jagr

153. Who was the first goaltender to score a goal in an NHL game?
a.   Martin Brodeur
b.   Ron Hextall
c.   Patrick Roy
d.   Billy Smith

154. What team was the first to win the Stanley Cup in the NHL era?
a.   Toronto Maple Leafs
b.   Montreal Canadiens
c.   Boston Bruins
d.   Chicago Blackhawks

155. Which player was the first to reach 1,000 career assists?
a.   Gordie Howe
b.   Wayne Gretzky

c. Ray Bourque
d. Mark Messier

156. Who was the first defenseman to win the Hart Memorial Trophy as the NHL's Most Valuable Player?
a. Bobby Orr
b. Ray Bourque
c. Nicklas Lidstrom
d. Denis Potvin

157. The fastest goal from the start of an NHL game was scored in how many seconds?
a. 5 seconds
b. 7 seconds
c. 9 seconds
d. 11 seconds

158. Which player holds the NHL record for most career hat tricks?
a. Mario Lemieux
b. Wayne Gretzky
c. Brett Hull
d. Mike Bossy

159. Who was the youngest captain in NHL history?
a. Sidney Crosby
b. Connor McDavid
c. Gabriel Landeskog
d. Jonathan Toews

160. Which team set the record for the longest winning streak in NHL history?
a. Pittsburgh Penguins
b. Detroit Red Wings
c. Philadelphia Flyers
d. Boston Bruins

161. Who is the only player to win four consecutive Stanley Cup Finals MVP awards?
a. Wayne Gretzky
b. Jean Beliveau
c. Mike Bossy
d. Maurice Richard

162. What year was the NHL founded?
a. 1909
b. 1917
c. 1926
d. 1931

163. Which team won the first Stanley Cup in 1893?
a. Montreal Canadiens
b. Montreal Amateur Athletic Association
c. Toronto Maple Leafs
d. Detroit Red Wings

164. Who is the only player to win the Conn Smythe Trophy (Playoff MVP) from a losing team?
a. Wayne Gretzky
b. Patrick Roy
c. Jean-Sebastien Giguere

d. Mario Lemieux

165. What team ended a 54-year Stanley Cup drought in 1994?
a. Boston Bruins
b. Chicago Blackhawks
c. New York Rangers
d. Toronto Maple Leafs

166. Which NHL team was the first to win back-to-back Stanley Cups in the expansion era (since 1967)?
a. Philadelphia Flyers
b. Montreal Canadiens
c. Pittsburgh Penguins
d. Edmonton Oilers

167. Who scored the Stanley Cup-winning goal in overtime for the Pittsburgh Penguins 2017?
a. Sidney Crosby
b. Evgeni Malkin
c. Patric Hornqvist
d. Kris Letang

168. What year did the Stanley Cup finals not occur due to a worldwide influenza epidemic?
a. 1919
b. 1945
c. 2005
d. 2020

169. Which team completed the most recent

"reverse sweep" (winning four straight after losing the first three games) in the Stanley Cup Finals?
a. Toronto Maple Leafs
b. Detroit Red Wings
c. New York Islanders
d. Los Angeles Kings

170. Who is the youngest captain ever to win the Stanley Cup?
a. Sidney Crosby
b. Jonathan Toews
c. Wayne Gretzky
d. Steve Yzerman

171. Which city's team won the Stanley Cup in its inaugural NHL season?
a. Las Vegas
b. St. Louis
c. Tampa Bay
d. Edmonton

172. Who was the first European-trained captain to lift the Stanley Cup?
a. Nicklas Lidstrom
b. Zdeno Chara c. Alex Ovechkin
c. Henrik Zetterberg

173. What team won the Stanley Cup during the 2004-2005 NHL lockout season?
a. None, the season was canceled
b. New Jersey Devils
c. Detroit Red Wings

d. Colorado Avalanche

174. Which player holds the record for most Stanley Cup wins as a player?
a. Maurice Richard
b. Wayne Gretzky
c. Henri Richard
d. Jean Beliveau

175. Which country won the first gold medal in Olympic ice hockey?
a. Canada
b. United States
c. Soviet Union
d. Sweden

176. Who was the first European player inducted into the Hockey Hall of Fame?
a. Jari Kurri b. Peter Stastny
b. Borje Salming
c. Vladislav Tretiak

177. The "Miracle on Ice" refers to the USA's upset victory over which team in the 1980 Winter Olympics?
a. Canada
b. Soviet Union
c. Sweden
d. Finland

178. Which country hosted the first Ice Hockey World Championships?
a. Switzerland
b. Canada
c. Czechoslovakia
d. France

179. Who was the first Russian player to captain an NHL Stanley Cup-winning team?
a. Alex Ovechkin
b. Pavel Datsyuk
c. Evgeni Malkin
d. Alexander Mogilny

180. Which nation won its first men's ice hockey gold at the Olympics in 1998?
a. Czech Republic
b. Slovakia
c. Finland
d. Russia

181. Who is considered the first excellent European star in the NHL?
a. Stan Mikita
b. Borje Salming
c. Peter Stastny
d. Sergei Fedorov

182. Which country's national team is known as "Tre Kronor" (Three Crowns)?
a. Finland
b. Sweden

c. Norway
d. Denmark

183. Who was the first Finnish player inducted into the Hockey Hall of Fame?
a. Teemu Selanne
b. Jari Kurri
c. Saku Koivu
d. Miikka Kiprusoff

184. The 1972 Summit Series was contested between Canada and which country?
a. United States
b. Soviet Union
c. Czechoslovakia
d. Sweden

185. Which country has the most medals in Olympic men's ice hockey?
a. Canada
b. Russia
c. United States
d. Sweden

186. Who was the first Czech player to win the Hart Memorial Trophy as the NHL's most valuable player?
a. Jaromir Jagr
b. Dominik Hasek
c. Peter Stastny
d. Pavel Bure

187. In what year did the NHL first allow its players to participate in the Winter Olympics?
a. 1988
b. 1992
c. 1998
d. 2002

188. When was the two-line pass rule eliminated from the NHL, encouraging more open play?
a. 1992
b. 1998
c. 2004
d. 2005

189. What year did the NHL introduce the shootout to resolve ties in regular-season games?
a. 1999
b. 2000
c. 2004
d. 2005

190. The NHL mandated the wearing of helmets by all players entering the league starting in what year?
a. 1979
b. 1982
c. 1987
d. 1990

191. When was the goalie trapezoid area behind the net introduced to limit goaltenders' puck-handling?
a. 1999
b. 2003
c. 2005
d. 2013

192. The offside rule was modified to allow the "tag-up" offside in what year, encouraging continuous play?
a. 1986
b. 1992
c. 2000
d. 2005

193. In what year did the NHL implement the "instigator rule," penalizing players who initiate fights?
a. 1978
b. 1985
c. 1992
d. 2005

194. When did the NHL first use video review to confirm goals?
a. 1986
b. 1991
c. 1999
d. 2003

195. The NHL adopted a three-on-three overtime format in what year to reduce the number of games decided by shootouts?
a. 2000
b. 2007
c. 2015
d. 2019

196. When was the "delayed penalty" rule introduced, allowing play to continue until the penalized team gains possession?
a. 1956
b. 1969
c. 1978
d. 1982

197. What year did the NHL begin requiring visors for all new players entering the league?
a. 2006
b. 2013
c. 2016
d. 2019

198. The NHL introduced the "Hybrid Icing" rule to enhance player safety in what season?
a. 2010-2011
b. 2012-2013
c. 2013-2014
d. 2015-2016

199. When were goal judges first moved from behind the nets to a higher position in arenas?
a. 1970
b. 1980
c. 1991
d. 2001

200. The "coach's challenge" for reviewing specific play calls was introduced in what year?
a. 2008
b. 2012
c. 2015
d. 2018

Combat Sports (Boxing & MMA)

201. Who did Muhammad Ali fight in the "Rumble in the Jungle"?
a. Joe Frazier
b. George Foreman
c. Sonny Liston
d. Ken Norton

202. In what year did Conor McGregor fight Floyd Mayweather in a boxing match?
a. 2015
b. 2016
c. 2017
d. 2018

203. Who was the first fighter to simultaneously hold UFC titles in two different weight classes?
a. Conor McGregor
b. Daniel Cormier
c. BJ Penn
d. Amanda Nunes

204. During his prime, which fighter was known as "The Baddest Man on the Planet"?
a. Mike Tyson
b. Evander Holyfield
c. Lennox Lewis
d. George Foreman

205. What legendary boxer was known for his "Philly Shell" defense?
a. Floyd Mayweather Jr.
b. Sugar Ray Leonard

c. Bernard Hopkins
d. Joe Frazier

206. Which MMA fighter executed a flying knee knockout just 5 seconds into the fight, setting a UFC record?
a. Jorge Masvidal
b. Conor McGregor
c. Anderson Silva
d. Jose Aldo

207. The "Thrilla in Manila" was the third and final fight between Muhammad Ali and whom?
a. Joe Frazier
b. Ken Norton
c. George Foreman
d. Sonny Liston

208. Who defeated Ronda Rousey to claim the UFC Women's Bantamweight Championship 2015?
a. Holly Holm
b. Amanda Nunes
c. Miesha Tate
d. Cris Cyborg

209. Which boxer moved from middleweight to light heavyweight to knock out Michael Moorer for the championship?
a. Roy Jones Jr.
b. Sugar Ray Robinson
c. Bernard Hopkins
d. Marvin Hagler

210. What MMA fighter is known for his "Stockton Slap"?
a.   Nate Diaz
b.   Nick Diaz
c.   Jorge Masvidal
d.   Conor McGregor

211. In which round did Mike Tyson bite Evander Holyfield's ear during their 1997 rematch?
a.   Round 1
b.   Round 2
c.   Round 3
d.   Round 5

212. Who was the first UFC fighter to defeat Anderson Silva in the UFC?
a.   Chris Weidman
b.   Michael Bisping
c.   Chael Sonnen
d.   Vitor Belfort

213. What iconic heavyweight boxing match is known for the phrase "Down goes Frazier!"?
a.   Muhammad Ali vs. Joe Frazier I
b.   George Foreman vs. Joe Frazier
c.   Muhammad Ali vs. George Foreman
d.   Joe Frazier vs. Ken Norton

214. Which MMA event marked the UFC debut of Brock Lesnar?
a.   UFC 69
b.   UFC 77

c. UFC 81
d. UFC 100

215. Gennady Golovkin is known for his knockout power in which weight class?
a. Welterweight
b. Middleweight
c. Light heavyweight
d. Heavyweight

216. Which boxer was famously imprisoned before returning to win a world title?
a. Mike Tyson
b. Floyd Mayweather Jr.
c. Sonny Liston
d. George Foreman

217. The "Bite Fight" involved Mike Tyson and which other boxer?
a. Evander Holyfield
b. Lennox Lewis
c. Riddick Bowe
d. Buster Douglas

218. Who faced a doping scandal before making a triumphant UFC return and regaining a title?
a. Jon Jones
b. Brock Lesnar
c. Anderson Silva
d. Georges St-Pierre

219. Which MMA fighter made a controversial

return from retirement, only to suffer a defeat in a boxing match against Floyd Mayweather Jr.?
a. Conor McGregor
b. Nate Diaz
c. Khabib Nurmagomedov
d. Nick Diaz

220. Who was involved in a controversial draw during their first fight, leading to a highly anticipated rematch?
a. Floyd Mayweather Jr. and Manny Pacquiao
b. Canelo Alvarez and Gennady Golovkin
c. Anthony Joshua and Andy Ruiz Jr.
d. Deontay Wilder and Tyson Fury

221. Which UFC fighter returned to win the Heavyweight Championship after battling diverticulitis?
a. Randy Couture
b. Brock Lesnar
c. Cain Velasquez
d. Stipe Miocic

222. The disqualification of which fighter led to one of the most controversial moments in UFC history?
a. Jon Jones
b. Daniel Cormier
c. Anderson Silva
d. Matt Hamill

223. Who made a controversial comeback to boxing at age 54 for an exhibition match in 2020?
a. Mike Tyson
b. Evander Holyfield
c. Roy Jones Jr.
d. Oscar De La Hoya

224. Which boxer was stripped of his titles following a doping scandal and mental health issues, before making a comeback to win the heavyweight championship again?
a. Anthony Joshua
b. Deontay Wilder
c. Tyson Fury
d. Vladimir Klitschko

225. The UFC 229 post-fight brawl involved which lightweight champion?
a. Conor McGregor
b. Khabib Nurmagomedov
c. Tony Ferguson
d. Dustin Poirier

226. Which fighter returned from a severe motorcycle accident to continue his boxing career?
a. Errol Spence Jr.
b. Manny Pacquiao
c. Keith Thurman
d. Shawn Porter

227. What controversial technique did Anderson Silva use against Demian Maia that led to widespread criticism?
a. Eye gouging
b. Taunting
c. Low blows
d. Fence grabbing

228. Who made a comeback to win the WBC Heavyweight Title at the age of 45?
a. George Foreman
b. Bernard Hopkins
c. Evander Holyfield
d. Larry Holmes

229. Which fighter's positive test for clomiphene overshadowed a highly anticipated rematch?
a. Jon Jones
b. Brock Lesnar
c. Canelo Alvarez
d. Dillian Whyte

230. After a dramatic loss and battling personal demons, which boxer returned victorious against Luis Ortiz?
a. Deontay Wilder
b. Tyson Fury
c. Anthony Joshua
d. Alexander Povetkin

231. What year was the first recorded prizefight in boxing history?
a. 1681
b. 1719
c. 1743
d. 1892

232. The Marquess of Queensberry Rules, which form the basis of modern boxing, were published in what year?
a. 1743
b. 1867
c. 1892
d. 1920

233. UFC 1, the event that marked the beginning of the UFC as a major MMA promotion, took place in what year?
a. 1989
b. 1993
c. 1999
d. 2001

234. Who is considered the father of modern Olympic Games and played a role in including boxing in the Olympics?
a. Pierre de Coubertin
b. Avery Brundage
c. Juan Antonio Samaranch
d. Jacques Rogge

235. The first women's MMA bout sanctioned by a US state athletic commission occurred in what year?
a. 1995
b. 1997
c. 2001
d. 2005

236. Which of these fighters is known as the "Father of American Jiu-Jitsu" and helped popularize Brazilian Jiu-Jitsu in the United States?
a. Royce Gracie
b. Ken Shamrock
c. Chuck Liddell
d. Randy Couture

237. In what year did women's boxing become an Olympic sport?
a. 2000
b. 2004
c. 2012
d. 2016

238. The "Brawl for All" was a controversial tournament held by WWE combining boxing and wrestling elements. It took place in which year?
a. 1995
b. 1998
c. 2000
d. 2002

239. Who was the first UFC fighter to be stripped of a title for disciplinary reasons, marking a significant moment in the sport's governance?
a. Jon Jones
b. Conor McGregor
c. Anderson Silva
d. Georges St-Pierre

240. In what year was the first instance of a "no holds barred" event recorded, which would later evolve into modern MMA?
a. 648 BC
b. 1776
c. 1887
d. 1920

241. Which country is credited with creating Muay Thai, also known as Thai boxing?
a. China
b. Japan
c. Thailand
d. Brazil

242. Who was the first female fighter inducted into the UFC Hall of Fame, marking a milestone in the recognition of women in the sport?
a. Ronda Rousey
b. Amanda Nunes
c. Cris Cyborg
d. Holly Holm

243. Which boxer's life story inspired the creation of the film "Raging Bull"?
a.   Jake LaMotta
b.   Rocky Marciano
c.   Muhammad Ali
d.   Joe Frazier

244. The UFC reality show that significantly boosted the sport's popularity is called what?
a.   Fight Night
b.   The Ultimate Fighter
c.   Knockout Kings
d.   MMA Masters

245. Which combat sports athlete starred in the movie "The Expendables"?
a.   Randy Couture
b.   Conor McGregor
c.   Ronda Rousey
d.   Floyd Mayweather

246. Muhammad Ali famously refused induction into the U.S. Army based on what grounds?
a.   Medical exemption
b.   Religious beliefs
c.   Opposition to war
d.   Personal beliefs against violence

247. Who is the boxer known for the phrase "Float like a butterfly, sting like a bee"?
a.   Mike Tyson
b.   Muhammad Ali

c. Floyd Mayweather Jr.
d. Manny Pacquiao

248. Which film series is credited with popularizing the underdog story in boxing?
a. Million Dollar Baby
b. Creed
c. Rocky
d. The Fighter

249. In what year did Ronda Rousey become the first woman to sign with the UFC, marking a significant moment for women in combat sports?
a. 2010
b. 2012
c. 2013
d. 2015

250. Which MMA fighter is known for his philanthropy work, particularly with children's hospitals in Brazil?
a. Anderson Silva
b. Georges St-Pierre
c. José Aldo
d. Conor McGregor

College Sports

251. The football rivalry between the University of Michigan and Ohio State University is famously known as what?
a. The Iron Bowl
b. The Big Game
c. The Red River Rivalry
d. The Game

252. Which two schools compete in the "Army-Navy Game," a celebrated college football rivalry?
a. United States Military Academy and United States Naval Academy
b. Texas A&M University and Virginia Military Institute
c. Air Force Academy and Coast Guard Academy
d. Citadel Military College and Norwich University

253. The annual football game between Harvard University and Yale University is known as what?
a. The Ivy League Showdown
b. The Academic Bowl
c. The Game
d. The Classic Duel

254. The "Iron Bowl" is a fierce rivalry between which two college football teams?
a. Alabama and Auburn
b. Georgia and Florida
c. Michigan and Ohio State
d. USC and UCLA

255. Which rivalry game is known as the "Red River Rivalry"?
a. Oklahoma vs. Texas
b. Nebraska vs. Oklahoma
c. Texas vs. Texas A&M
d. Kansas vs. Missouri

256. The "Holy War" refers to the football rivalry between which two universities?
a. Notre Dame and Boston College
b. BYU and Utah
c. Notre Dame and USC
d. Boston College and Harvard

257. Which rivalry is called the "Civil War" in college sports?
a. Oregon vs. Oregon State
b. Harvard vs. Yale
c. USC vs. Notre Dame
d. Florida vs. Georgia

258. The rivalry between the University of Florida and the University of Georgia is colloquially known as what?
a. The Sunshine Showdown
b. The Cocktail Party
c. The Border War
d. The Southern Clash

259. The "Backyard Brawl" is a historic rivalry between which two college football teams?
a. Penn State vs. Ohio State

b. West Virginia vs. Pittsburgh
c. Alabama vs. LSU
d. Texas vs. Texas A&M

260. The "Bayou Classic" is an annual football game that features which two teams?
a. LSU and Tulane
b. Grambling State and Southern University
c. University of Florida and University of Miami
d. Alabama State and Alabama A&M

261. Which two teams compete in the "Paul Bunyan Trophy" game?
a. Minnesota and Wisconsin
b. Michigan and Ohio State
c. Michigan and Michigan State
d. Purdue and Indiana

262. The "Floyd of Rosedale" trophy is contested between which two college football teams?
a. Iowa and Minnesota
b. Oklahoma and Nebraska
c. Texas and Arkansas
d. California and Stanford

263. Which university won the first NCAA Division I men's basketball championship in 1939?
a. University of Oregon
b. Indiana University
c. University of Kansas
d. University of North Carolina

264. Who hit the game-winning shot for North Carolina in the 1982 NCAA men's basketball championship?
a. Michael Jordan
b. James Worthy
c. Sam Perkins
d. Dean Smith

265. The University of Connecticut's women's basketball team completed an undefeated season and won the national championship in 1995 under which head coach?
a. Pat Summitt
b. Geno Auriemma
c. Tara VanDerveer
d. Muffet McGraw

266. Which team broke UCLA's record of 7 consecutive NCAA men's basketball championships by winning in 1977?
a. Indiana Hoosiers
b. Marquette Warriors
c. Kentucky Wildcats
d. North Carolina State Wolfpack

267. Who scored the "Miracle Minute" points for Duke against Maryland in 2001, leading to a comeback win?
a. Jay Williams
b. Shane Battier
c. J.J. Redick
d. Christian Laettner

268. In what year did the Texas Longhorns win the NCAA Division I Football Championship with Vince Young as their quarterback?
a. 2002
b. 2005
c. 2008
d. 2010

269. The "Flutie Effect" is attributed to a Hail Mary pass thrown by Doug Flutie in 1984 for which college team?
a. Notre Dame Fighting Irish
b. Boston College Eagles
c. Miami Hurricanes
d. Michigan Wolverines

270. Which women's college softball team won the Women's College World Series with a walk-off grand slam in 2017?
a. University of Florida
b. University of Oklahoma
c. University of Arizona
d. University of Alabama

271. Villanova's Kris Jenkins hit a buzzer-beater to win the NCAA men's basketball championship in what year?
a. 2014
b. 2016
c. 2018
d. 2020

272. In 2007, Appalachian State University football team, competing in the FCS, defeated which FBS team, marking one of the biggest upsets in college football history?
a. University of Michigan
b. Ohio State University
c. University of Alabama
d. University of Texas

273. Who led the LSU Tigers to the 2019 College Football Playoff National Championship as quarterback?
a. Joe Burrow
b. Trevor Lawrence
c. Tua Tagovailoa
d. Justin Fields

274. Which college won the first NCAA Women's Volleyball Championship in 1981?
a. Stanford University
b. University of Southern California
c. University of Nebraska
d. University of Texas

275. What team did Notre Dame defeat to win the 1988 NCAA Division I Football National Championship?
a. West Virginia Mountaineers
b. Miami Hurricanes
c. Colorado Buffaloes
d. Alabama Crimson Tide

276. Which university's men's ice hockey team completed a perfect season by winning the NCAA championship in 1970?
a. University of Michigan
b. Boston University
c. Cornell University
d. University of North Dakota

277. Who is the only coach to win an NCAA football national championship and a Super Bowl?
a. Nick Saban
b. Urban Meyer
c. Pete Carroll
d. Jimmy Johnson

278. Which college did basketball star Zion Williamson attend before joining the NBA?
a. Duke University
b. University of North Carolina
c. Kentucky University
d. UCLA

279. Olympic gold medalist and World Cup champion soccer player Alex Morgan played for which university?
a. Stanford University
b. University of California, Berkeley
c. University of Southern California
d. University of North Carolina at Chapel Hill

280. Simone Biles, a world-renowned gymnast, committed to which university before turning

professional?
a. University of Florida
b. UCLA
c. University of Alabama
d. Ohio State University

281. Heisman Trophy winner Joe Burrow played quarterback for which college before leading LSU to a national championship?
a. Ohio State University
b. University of Michigan
c. University of Alabama
d. University of Florida

282. Basketball Hall of Famer and cultural icon Michael Jordan played college basketball for which school?
a. Duke University
b. University of North Carolina at Chapel Hill
c. Indiana University
d. University of Kentucky

283. NFL star quarterback Russell Wilson played college football for NC State before transferring to which university for his final year?
a. University of Wisconsin
b. University of Michigan
c. Ohio State University
d. Stanford University

284. Which university did Heisman Trophy winner and MLB/NFL athlete Bo Jackson attend?

a. Auburn University
b. University of Alabama
c. University of Georgia
d. Louisiana State University

285. Before his NBA career, Stephen Curry played college basketball for which university?
a. Davidson College
b. Duke University
c. University of North Carolina at Chapel Hill
d. Virginia Tech

286. NFL wide receiver Julio Jones played college football at which university?
a. University of Georgia
b. University of Alabama
c. Auburn University
d. Louisiana State University

287. Legendary NFL quarterback Peyton Manning played college football for which SEC school?
a. University of Tennessee
b. University of Florida
c. University of Georgia
d. University of Alabama

288. Which university students camp in a tent village known as "Krzyzewskiville" for basketball tickets?
a. University of Kentucky
b. Duke University

c. University of North Carolina
d. Indiana University

289. The "World's Largest Outdoor Cocktail Party" is the nickname for the annual football game between which two universities?
a. University of Texas and University of Oklahoma
b. University of Michigan and Ohio State University
c. University of Georgia and University of Florida
d. University of Alabama and Auburn University

290. The "Sod Cemetery" celebrates away game victories for which college football team?
a. Florida State University
b. University of Miami
c. Clemson University
d. University of Notre Dame

291. What unique item is thrown onto the ice at the University of Michigan's hockey games after the first goal?
a. Rubber chickens
b. Stuffed animals
c. Octopi
d. Tennis balls

292. "Midnight Yell" is a tradition at which university's football games?
a. Texas A&M University
b. University of Nebraska

c. Penn State University
d. University of Southern California

293. Which university's band performs the "Script Ohio" formation during football games?
a. Ohio State University
b. University of Michigan
c. Indiana University
d. University of Iowa

294. At which university do students participate in the "Tortilla Toss" at football games?
a. Texas Tech University
b. University of Texas at Austin
c. Baylor University
d. Texas Christian University

295. Which university's football fans perform a "Haka" dance before games?
a. University of Hawaii
b. Brigham Young University
c. University of Utah
d. San Diego State University

296. The "Running of the Bulls" is a tradition for which university's football team?
a. University of South Florida
b. University of Colorado Boulder
c. University of Alabama
d. University of Texas

**297. Which university is known for its "Senior

Walk," where the names of all graduates are engraved on campus sidewalks?
a. Harvard University
b. University of Arkansas
c. Stanford University
d. University of Michigan

298. The "Fifth Quarter" is a post-game musical tradition performed by which university's marching band?
a. University of Wisconsin
b. Ohio State University
c. University of Michigan
d. Penn State University

299. Which university's football tradition involves touching a "Play Like a Champion Today" sign before games?
a. University of Notre Dame
b. University of Oklahoma
c. University of Southern California
d. University of Miami

300. The tradition of "Jump Around" between the third and fourth quarters is celebrated by fans of which university's football team?
a. University of Iowa
b. University of Wisconsin
c. Michigan State University
d. University of Nebraska

Olympics

301. Who became the most decorated Olympian at the London 2012 Olympics?
a. Mark Spitz
b. Carl Lewis
c. Michael Phelps
d. Simone Biles

302. Which American gymnast was the first to win the individual all-around gold at the Olympics and World Championships?
a. Simone Biles
b. Gabby Douglas
c. Mary Lou Retton
d. Nastia Liukin

303. Who broke the world record for the 100m sprint at the 1968 Mexico City Olympics?
a. Carl Lewis
b. Jesse Owens
c. Jim Hines
d. Usain Bolt

304. Which American athlete won four gold medals in long jump over four Olympic Games?
a. Jackie Joyner-Kersee
b. Carl Lewis
c. Mike Powell
d. Bob Beamon

305. Who is the first American woman to win three gold medals in track and field at a single Olympics?
a. Florence Griffith Joyner

b. Wilma Rudolph
c. Allyson Felix
d. Betty Cuthbert

306. In which Olympics did swimmer Mark Spitz win seven gold medals?
a. Munich 1972
b. Mexico City 1968
c. Montreal 1976 d. Los Angeles 1984

307. Who was the youngest male American swimmer to win a gold medal at the Olympics?
a. Michael Phelps
b. Mark Spitz
c. Ryan Lochte
d. Caeleb Dressel

308. Which American figure skater won the ladies' singles Olympic gold in 1968?
a. Peggy Fleming
b. Dorothy Hamill
c. Kristi Yamaguchi
d. Tara Lipinski

309. Who was the first American to win the Olympic marathon?
a. Frank Shorter
b. Meb Keflezighi
c. Joan Benoit
d. Billy Mills

310. Shaun White is known for winning gold medals in which Winter Olympic sport?
a. Skiing
b. Snowboarding
c. Figure Skating
d. Bobsleigh

311. Which American Olympian is known for their "Fosbury Flop" high jump technique?
a. Dick Fosbury
b. Charles Austin
c. Javier Sotomayor
d. Bob Beamon

312. Who was the first American woman to win an Olympic medal in judo?
a. Kayla Harrison
b. Ronda Rousey
c. Marti Malloy
d. AnnMaria De Mars

313. At the 2008 Beijing Olympics, which American female swimmer won six medals?
a. Katie Ledecky
b. Missy Franklin
c. Natalie Coughlin
d. Dara Torres

314. Lindsey Vonn won her Olympic gold in what event at the Vancouver 2010 Winter Olympics?
a. Super-G
b. Downhill

c. Giant Slalom
d. Slalom

315. In which city were the first modern Olympic Games held in 1896?
a. Paris, France
b. Athens, Greece
c. London, England
d. Berlin, Germany

316. The 1936 Summer Olympics, known for Jesse Owens' outstanding performance, were held in which city?
a. Los Angeles, USA
b. Berlin, Germany
c. Tokyo, Japan
d. London, England

317. Which Olympics was the first to include female athletes?
a. 1900 Paris Olympics
b. 1912 Stockholm Olympics
c. 1920 Antwerp Olympics
d. 1928 Amsterdam Olympics

318. The "Miracle on Ice," where the USA ice hockey team defeated the Soviet Union, occurred during the Winter Olympics of which year?
a. 1972
b. 1980
c. 1984
d. 1988

319. Which city hosted the Summer Olympics twice in the 20th century, once in 1932 and again in 1984?
a. Paris, France
b. Los Angeles, USA
c. London, England
d. Tokyo, Japan

320. The 1972 Munich Olympics were overshadowed by what tragic event?
a. A boycott by multiple countries
b. The Munich massacre
c. A natural disaster
d. A doping scandal

321. Which city was the first in Asia to host the Olympic Games?
a. Beijing, China
b. Tokyo, Japan
c. Seoul, South Korea
d. Bangkok, Thailand

322. Which year were the first Winter Olympics held?
a. 1912
b. 1924
c. 1936
d. 1948

323. Which city's Olympics featured Muhammad Ali lighting the Olympic cauldron in 1996?
a. Atlanta, USA
b. Sydney, Australia

c. Athens, Greece
d. Beijing, China

324. The first Olympic Games to be broadcast live on television took place in which city?
a. Rome, Italy
b. Tokyo, Japan
c. Mexico City, Mexico
d. London, England

325. Which city hosted the Summer Olympics where women's boxing was included for the first time?
a. Beijing, China
b. Athens, Greece
c. London, England
d. Rio de Janeiro, Brazil

326. The first Paralympic Games were held immediately following the 1960 Summer Olympics in which city?
a. Rome, Italy
b. Tokyo, Japan
c. London, England
d. Paris, France

327. The Olympic flame was lit by an archer shooting a flaming arrow for the first time during the opening ceremony of which Olympics?
a. Seoul 1988
b. Barcelona 1992
c. Atlanta 1996

d. Sydney 2000

328. During the 1968 Mexico City Olympics, which two athletes performed the Black Power salute?
a. Jesse Owens and Ralph Metcalfe
b. Tommie Smith and John Carlos
c. Carl Lewis and Joe DeLoach
d. Usain Bolt and Yohan Blake

329. Which Olympics were boycotted by the United States and several other countries due to the Soviet invasion of Afghanistan?
a. 1976 Montreal
b. 1980 Moscow
c. 1984 Los Angeles
d. 1988 Seoul

330. At which Olympic Games did North and South Korea march together under a unified flag for the first time?
a. Sydney 2000
b. Athens 2004
c. Beijing 2008
d. Pyeongchang 2018

331. The disqualification of which sprinter for doping was a major controversy at the 1988 Seoul Olympics?
a. Carl Lewis
b. Ben Johnson
c. Linford Christie
d. Flo-Jo (Florence Griffith Joyner)

332. Which figure skater was involved in a controversy leading up to the 1994 Winter Olympics, including an attack on a fellow competitor?
a.   Nancy Kerrigan
b.   Tonya Harding
c.   Katarina Witt
d.   Michelle Kwan

333. In what year did the Olympic Games first allow professional athletes to compete, breaking a long-standing tradition of amateurism?
a.   1984 Los Angeles
b.   1988 Seoul
c.   1992 Barcelona
d.   1996 Atlanta

334. The "Blood in the Water" match, a water polo game that turned violent, was between Hungary and which country at the 1956 Melbourne Olympics?
a.   Soviet Union
b.   United States
c.   Australia
d.   Yugoslavia

335. Which Olympic Games featured the first all-refugee team to compete?
a.   London 2012
b.   Rio 2016
c.   Pyeongchang 2018
d.   Tokyo 2020

336. In which Olympics did Greg Louganis hit his head on the springboard during a dive but still went on to win gold?
a. 1984 Los Angeles
b. 1988 Seoul
c. 1992 Barcelona
d. 1996 Atlanta

337. Who became the first transgender woman to compete in the Olympic Games, participating in weightlifting at Tokyo 2020?
a. Caitlyn Jenner
b. Fallon Fox
c. Laurel Hubbard
d. Caster Semenya

338. Which country's women's soccer team wore hijabs for the first time in Olympic competition during the London 2012 Games?
a. Iran
b. Saudi Arabia
c. Egypt
d. Afghanistan

339. Which year's Olympics featured the iconic Black Power salute on the medal podium?
a. 1964 Tokyo
b. 1968 Mexico City
c. 1972 Munich
d. 1980 Moscow

340. In which Olympics did the "Miracle on Ice,"

where the US ice hockey team defeated the Soviet Union, occur?
a. 1976 Innsbruck
b. 1980 Lake Placid
c. 1984 Sarajevo
d. 1988 Calgary

341. Who became the first openly transgender athlete to compete at the Olympics in Tokyo in 2020?
a. Caitlyn Jenner
b. Chelsea Wolfe
c. Laurel Hubbard
d. Quinn

342. Which Olympics were boycotted by 65 nations due to the host country's invasion of Afghanistan?
a. 1976 Montreal
b. 1980 Moscow
c. 1984 Los Angeles
d. 1988 Seoul

343. At which Olympics did North and South Korean athletes march together under a unified flag for the first time?
a. 2000 Sydney
b. 2004 Athens
c. 2018 Pyeongchang
d. 2020 Tokyo

344. During which Olympics did the Israeli Olympic team suffer a tragic terrorist attack?

a. 1968 Mexico City
b. 1972 Munich
c. 1976 Montreal
d. 1984 Los Angeles

345. Which country's women's soccer team protested inequality by wearing purple ribbons during the Tokyo 2020 Olympics?
a. United States
b. Brazil
c. Sweden
d. Canada

346. In which year did the Olympic Games first feature athletes from every competing nation in the opening ceremony's Parade of Nations?
a. 1920 Antwerp
b. 1956 Melbourne
c. 1964 Tokyo
d. 1980 Moscow

347. Who was the first female Muslim American athlete to wear a hijab while competing in the Olympics, doing so in Rio 2016?
a. Dalilah Muhammad
b. Ibtihaj Muhammad
c. Sarah Attar
d. Tahmina Kohistani

348. The Rio 2016 Olympics saw which two countries' athletes take selfies together, symbolizing peace despite their nations' conflict?

a. North Korea and South Korea
b. India and Pakistan
c. Israel and Palestine
d. Russia and Ukraine

349. Which athlete carried the Refugee Olympic Team flag at the Rio 2016 Olympics opening ceremony?
a. Yusra Mardini
b. Rose Nathike Lokonyen
c. James Chiengjiek
d. Yiech Pur Biel

350. During which Olympics did a gymnast perform with a broken leg to secure gold for her team?
a. 1976 Montreal
b. 1984 Los Angeles
c. 1996 Atlanta
d. 2008 Beijing

Soccer

351. Which U.S. city was the first to host a Major League Soccer (MLS) game in 1996?
a. Los Angeles, California
b. San Jose, California
c. New York, New York
d. Seattle, Washington

352. Who did Major League Soccer sign the first player in 1995?
a. Landon Donovan
b. Tab Ramos
c. David Beckham
d. Alexi Lalas

353. The United States hosted the FIFA World Cup in what year?
a. 1986
b. 1990
c. 1994
d. 1998

354. Which U.S. women's national team player scored the winning penalty in the 1999 FIFA Women's World Cup Final?
a. Mia Hamm
b. Brandi Chastain
c. Julie Foudy
d. Kristine Lilly

355. The U.S. Men's National Team made it to the quarterfinals of the FIFA World Cup in which year?
a.   1994
b.   2002
c.   2010
d.   2014

356. Who is the all-time leading U.S. Men's National Soccer Team scorer?
a.   Clint Dempsey
b.   Landon Donovan
c.   Jozy Altidore
d.   Brian McBride

357. The first soccer-specific stadium built for an MLS team in the United States is in which city?
a.   Columbus, Ohio
b.   Carson, California
c.   Harrison, New Jersey
d.   Frisco, Texas

358. Who was the first major international star to sign with Major League Soccer, boosting its global profile?
a.   Thierry Henry
b.   David Beckham
c.   Kaká
d.   Andrea Pirlo

359. Which team won the inaugural MLS Cup in 1996?
a. D.C. United
b. LA Galaxy
c. New York/New Jersey MetroStars
d. Colorado Rapids

360. In what year did the U.S. Women's National Soccer Team win their first FIFA Women's World Cup?
a. 1991
b. 1999
c. 2015
d. 2019

361. The U.S. Men's National Team's stunning victory over England in the 1950 FIFA World Cup is known as the:
a. Miracle Match
b. Game of the Century
c. Historic Upset
d. Belo Horizonte Miracle

362. What year did Major League Soccer introduce the Designated Player Rule, often called the "Beckham Rule"?
a. 2005
b. 2007
c. 2010
d. 2012

363. Which match is "The Miracle of Istanbul," where Liverpool FC returned from a 3-0 halftime deficit to win the UEFA Champions League in 2005?
a. Liverpool vs. AC Milan
b. Liverpool vs. Real Madrid
c. Liverpool vs. Manchester United
d. Liverpool vs. FC Barcelona

364. In the 2014 FIFA World Cup, Germany defeated Brazil 7-1 in a match in which Brazilian city?
a. Rio de Janeiro
b. São Paulo
c. Belo Horizonte
d. Salvador

365. The "Hand of God" goal by Diego Maradona occurred during the 1986 World Cup quarter-final match between Argentina and which team?
a. Brazil
b. England
c. Italy
d. West Germany

366. The 1950 FIFA World Cup final, which saw Uruguay defeat Brazil in Rio de Janeiro, is referred to as what?
a. The Maracanazo
b. The Miracle Match
c. The Shock of the Century
d. The Ultimate Upset

367. Which match is known for Zinedine Zidane's headbutt in the 2006 FIFA World Cup Final?
a. France vs. Italy
b. France vs. Brazil
c. France vs. Portugal
d. France vs. Spain

368. In what year did Manchester United complete a dramatic comeback to win the UEFA Champions League in injury time against Bayern Munich?
a. 1999
b. 2001
c. 2008
d. 2012

369. The first ever FIFA World Cup Final in 1930 was contested between which countries?
a. Argentina vs. Uruguay
b. Brazil vs. Italy
c. Germany vs. Netherlands
d. Spain vs. England

370. The "Battle of Santiago" refers to a notoriously violent match during the 1962 World Cup between Italy and which other team?
a. Chile
b. Brazil
c. England
d. Argentina

371. Which team won the UEFA Euro 2004,

considered one of the biggest surprises in the tournament's history?
a. Greece
b. Portugal
c. Spain
d. France

372. The 2012 UEFA Champions League Final saw Chelsea FC win their first Champions League title against which team?
a. Manchester United
b. FC Barcelona
c. Bayern Munich
d. Real Madrid

373. In 2018, which country won its second FIFA World Cup, 20 years after their first victory?
a. France
b. Brazil
c. Germany
d. Argentina

374. Which game is famously known as "The Dentist's Chair" match during Euro 1996, involving England and which other team?
a. Scotland
b. Germany
c. Netherlands
d. Spain

**375. Who is the only player to have won three FIFA

World Cups?
a. Lionel Messi
b. Cristiano Ronaldo
c. Pelé
d. Diego Maradona

376. Which player has won the most Ballon d'Or awards?
a. Michel Platini
b. Johan Cruyff
c. Lionel Messi
d. Cristiano Ronaldo

377. Who scored a record 16 goals across four FIFA World Cup tournaments?
a. Ronaldo
b. Miroslav Klose
c. Gerd Müller
d. Just Fontaine

378. Which female player has won FIFA World Player of the Year six times?
a. Abby Wambach
b. Marta
c. Mia Hamm
d. Birgit Prinz

379. Who became the first English player to win league titles in four countries?
a. David Beckham
b. Kevin Keegan
c. Gary Lineker

d. Frank Lampard

380. Which player was "El Pibe de Oro" (The Golden Boy)?
a. Lionel Messi
b. Diego Maradona
c. Zinedine Zidane
d. Ronaldinho

381. Who was the first player to score in four UEFA Champions League finals?
a. Cristiano Ronaldo
b. Lionel Messi
c. Raúl
d. Alfredo Di Stéfano

382. Which player is known for inventing the "Cruyff Turn"?
a. Johan Cruyff
b. Franz Beckenbauer
c. George Best
d. Pelé

383. Who was the top scorer in the inaugural Premier League season (1992-1993)?
a. Alan Shearer
b. Eric Cantona
c. Teddy Sheringham
d. Ian Wright

384. Who was named FIFA's Best Men's Player of

the 20th Century alongside Pelé?
a. Diego Maradona
b. Johan Cruyff
c. Franz Beckenbauer
d. Alfredo Di Stéfano

385. Which player led France to victory in the 1998 World Cup and Euro 2000?
a. Thierry Henry
b. Michel Platini
c. Zinedine Zidane
d. Didier Deschamps

386. Who was the first African player to be named FIFA World Player of the Year?
a. George Weah
b. Samuel Eto'o
c. Didier Drogba
d. Yaya Touré

387. Which player holds the record for the fastest hat-trick in the Premier League?
a. Robbie Fowler
b. Alan Shearer
c. Sergio Agüero
d. Sadio Mané

388. Which country's football league is known for its "Jogo Bonito" style, emphasizing skillful, attacking soccer?
a. Spain
b. Brazil

c. Italy
d. England

389. The "Superclásico" is a fierce soccer rivalry in Argentina between which two teams?
a. River Plate and Boca Juniors
b. Independiente and Racing Club
c. San Lorenzo and Huracán
d. Rosario Central and Newell's Old Boys

390. Which soccer club is known for its foundation rooted in anti-fascism, social justice, and community involvement, particularly in its supporter culture?
a. Manchester United
b. FC Barcelona
c. St. Pauli
d. Olympique de Marseille

391. The annual international tournament "Copa Libertadores" is contested by clubs from which continent?
a. Europe
b. South America
c. North America
d. Africa

392. "Calcio Storico" is a traditional event in which city, blending historical elements of soccer, rugby, and wrestling?
a. Rome, Italy
b. Florence, Italy

c. Venice, Italy
d. Milan, Italy

393. Which country's national team is nicknamed "The Indomitable Lions"?
a. Nigeria
b. Cameroon
c. Senegal
d. Ivory Coast

394. The "Ceasefire Game" during World War I, where soldiers from opposing sides played soccer, occurred on Christmas Day. Which year did it occur?
a. 1914
b. 1915
c. 1916
d. 1917

395. Which Japanese soccer player is known for significantly influencing the popularity of soccer in Asia and Europe through his international career?
a. Keisuke Honda
b. Shinji Kagawa
c. Hidetoshi Nakata
d. Kazuyoshi Miura

396. The "Old Firm" derby in Scotland features which two football clubs, known for their historic and cultural rivalry?
a. Aberdeen and Dundee United
b. Hearts and Hibernian

c. Celtic and Rangers
d. Kilmarnock and Motherwell

397. Which African country's success in the 1990 FIFA World Cup helped raise the profile of African soccer on the world stage?
a. Nigeria
b. Cameroon
c. Ghana
d. Egypt

398. "Futbol de Barrio" (Neighborhood Football) is a community-focused soccer initiative primarily associated with which country?
a. Mexico
b. Spain
c. Brazil
d. Argentina

399. The first country outside of Europe to win a FIFA World Cup was?
a. Argentina
b. Brazil
c. Uruguay
d. Mexico

400. The Premier League's introduction of the "No Room for Racism" campaign was aimed at combating what issue within soccer?
a. Match-fixing
b. Racism
c. Doping

d.   Hooliganism

★★★★★

SHARE YOUR THOUGHTS!

Dear Reader,

As the author, I find your feedback invaluable. Your insights and opinions enhance my understanding of this book's impact and significantly influence my future work! Please consider leaving an honest review because your feedback guides other readers and helps us grow.

How to Leave a Review

Scan the QR code, which will take you to the review page.

Your voice matters. Lend it to the conversation and help shape future reads!

Thank you.

Answers

1. b. Wilt Chamberlain
2. b. George Mikan
3. b. Earl Lloyd
4. b. Kenny Sailors
5. c. Nate Thurmond
6. c. Wilt Chamberlain
7. b. Ann Meyers
8. a. Red Auerbach
9. a. Bob Pettit
10. a. Chuck Cooper
11. d. Paul Pressey
12. c. Stephen Curry
13. a. 1989
14. b. Michael Jordan
15. b. Los Angeles Clippers
16. a. Kawhi Leonard
17. c. Celtics' Cedric Maxwell urged teammates to "hop on my back"
18. b. 2015-16 Golden State Warriors
19. c. Utah Jazz
20. a. Damian Lillard
21. b. Michael Jordan
22. a. Detroit Pistons
23. b. 2013
24. d. Wilt Chamberlain
25. a. 55
26. c. John Stockton
27. d. Jim Tucker
28. b. LeBron James
29. c. Kareem Abdul-Jabbar
30. c. John Stockton
31. c. 14
32. b. Michael Jordan
33. d. 17
34. a. Wilt Chamberlain
35. b. Wilt Chamberlain
36. b. Russell Westbrook
37. a. United States
38. a. Dirk Nowitzki
39. a. Yugoslavia
40. a. Yao Ming
41. a. 1936
42. b. Angola
43. c. Pau Gasol
44. a. Buenos Aires, Argentina
45. c. Hakeem Olajuwon
46. b. New Zealand
47. b. FIBA Asia Cup
48. b. Oscar Schmidt

49. a. Soviet Union
50. a. Yao Ming
51. a. 1876
52. b. Alexander Cartwright
53. a. Hoboken, New Jersey
54. b. Boston Red Sox
55. a. 1869
56. a. The first professional baseball team was formed
57. d. Morgan Bulkeley
58. a. New York City
59. b. 1901
60. d. The baseball diamond
61. a. New York Nine and Knickerbocker Club
62. b. Alexander Cartwright
63. c. Lou Gehrig
64. a. Hank Aaron
65. b. Murderers' Row
66. c. Ichiro Suzuki
67. b. Jackie Robinson
68. a. Boston Red Sox
69. a. Yogi Berra
70. b. Sammy Sosa
71. a. Nolan Ryan
72. c. Bobby Thomson
73. a. Frank Robinson
74. b. Boston Red Sox
75. a. New York Mets
76. a. Arizona Diamondbacks
77. c. Bobby Thomson
78. a. 2016
79. b. Manny Ramirez
80. a. 1989 World Series
81. a. Chicago Cubs
82. a. Washington Nationals
83. a. 1977 World Series
84. b. Don Larsen
85. a. Boston Red Sox
86. a. 1969
87. a. Atlanta Braves
88. a. Washington Nationals

89. d. A train that moves when a home run is hit
90. c. Mickey Mantle
91. c. Wrigley Field
92. a. 1976
93. d. Black Cat
94. a. Wade Boggs
95. a. .200
96. b. Octopus
97. a. Bert Campaneris
98. d. Tortillas
99. c. Vladimir Guerrero
100. a. Atlanta Braves
101. b. 1920
102. c. 1967
103. d. Gallaudet University
104. a. 1906
105. a. Walter Camp
106. b. George Halas
107. b. Moving the goalposts to the back of the end zone
108. b. 1970
109. a. Art Shell
110. a. 1986
111. b. Cincinnati Bengals
112. b. 1970
113. c. Bart Starr
114. a. Jerry Rice
115. b. Randy White
116. c. Tom Brady
117. b. Dallas Cowboys
118. a. Lynn Swann
119. b. Pittsburgh Steelers
120. b. John Elway
121. a. Rod Martin
122. a. Adam Vinatieri
123. b. Bart Starr
124. a. Bill Belichick
125. b. Bill Walsh
126. a. Buddy Ryan
127. b. Sam Wyche
128. a. Don Coryell
129. a. Tony Dungy
130. b. Jim Harbaugh
131. a. Bill Parcells
132. a. Tony Sparano
133. a. Pete Carroll
134. a. Marv Levy
135. a. Tom Landry
136. a. Bill Cowher
137. b. Mike Martz
138. a. Seattle Seahawks
139. a. Green Bay Packers

140. a. Las Vegas Raiders
141. d. Plastic Turkeys
142. a. Green Bay Packers
143. a. Pittsburgh Steelers
144. a. New Orleans Saints
145. a. Cleveland Browns
146. a. Buffalo Bills
147. b. Kansas City Chiefs
148. a. Minnesota Vikings
149. a. Buffalo Bills
150. a. New York Jets
151. b. Maurice Richard
152. b. Wayne Gretzky
153. d. Billy Smith
154. b. Montreal Canadiens
155. b. Wayne Gretzky
156. a. Bobby Orr
157. a. 5 seconds
158. b. Wayne Gretzky
159. c. Gabriel Landeskog
160. b. Detroit Red Wings
161. c. Mike Bossy
162. b. 1917
163. b. Montreal Amateur Athletic Association
164. c. Jean-Sebastien Giguere
165. c. New York Rangers
166. a. Philadelphia Flyers
167. c. Patric Hornqvist
168. a. 1919
169. d. Los Angeles Kings
170. b. Jonathan Toews
171. c. Tampa Bay
172. a. Nicklas Lidstrom
173. a. None, the season was canceled
174. c. Henri Richard
175. a. Canada
176. c. Borje Salming
177. b. Soviet Union

178.d. France
179.a. Alex Ovechkin
180.a. Czech Republic
181.a. Stan Mikita
182.b. Sweden
183.b. Jari Kurri
184.b. Soviet Union
185.a. Canada
186.b. Dominik Hasek
187.c. 1998
188.d. 2005
189.d. 2005
190.a. 1979
191.c. 2005
192.a. 1986
193.c. 1992
194.b. 1991
195.c. 2015
196.a. 1956
197.b. 2013
198.c. 2013-2014
199.c. 1991
200.c. 2015
201.b. George Foreman
202.c. 2017
203.a. Conor McGregor
204.a. Mike Tyson
205.a. Floyd Mayweather Jr.
206.a. Jorge Masvidal
207.a. Joe Frazier
208.a. Holly Holm
209.c. Bernard Hopkins
210.a. Nate Diaz
211.c. Round 3
212.a. Chris Weidman
213.b. George Foreman vs. Joe Frazier
214.c. UFC 81
215.b. Middleweight
216.a. Mike Tyson
217.a. Evander Holyfield
218.a. Jon Jones
219.a. Conor McGregor
220.b. Canelo Alvarez and Gennady Golovkin
221.b. Brock Lesnar
222.a. Jon Jones
223.a. Mike Tyson
224.c. Tyson Fury
225.b. Khabib Nurmagomedov

226.a. Errol Spence Jr.
227.b. Taunting
228.a. George Foreman
229.b. Brock Lesnar
230.b. Tyson Fury
231.a. 1681
232.b. 1867
233.b. 1993
234.a. Pierre de Coubertin
235.b. 1997
236.a. Royce Gracie
237.c. 2012
238.b. 1998
239.a. Jon Jones
240.a. 648 BC
241.c. Thailand
242.a. Ronda Rousey
243.a. Jake LaMotta
244.b. The Ultimate Fighter
245.a. Randy Couture
246.b. Religious beliefs
247.b. Muhammad Ali
248.c. Rocky
249.b. 2012
250.a. Anderson Silva
251.d. The Game
252.a. United States Military Academy and United States Naval Academy
253.c. The Game
254.a. Alabama and Auburn
255.a. Oklahoma vs. Texas
256.b. BYU and Utah
257.a. Oregon vs. Oregon State
258.b. The Cocktail Party
259.b. West Virginia vs. Pittsburgh
260.b. Grambling State and Southern University
261.c. Michigan and Michigan State
262.a. Iowa and Minnesota
263.a. University of Oregon
264.a. Michael Jordan
265.b. Geno Auriemma
266.b. Marquette Warriors
267.a. Jay Williams
268.b. 2005

269.b. Boston College Eagles
270.b. University of Oklahoma
271.b. 2016
272.a. University of Michigan
273.a. Joe Burrow
274.b. University of Southern California
275.a. West Virginia Mountaineers
276.c. Cornell University
277.d. Jimmy Johnson
278.a. Duke University
279.b. University of California, Berkeley
280.b. UCLA
281.a. Ohio State University
282.b. University of North Carolina at Chapel Hill
283.a. University of Wisconsin
284.a. Auburn University
285.a. Davidson College
286.b. University of Alabama
287.a. University of Tennessee
288.b. Duke University
289.c. University of Georgia and University of Florida
290.a. Florida State University
291.d. Tennis balls
292.a. Texas A&M University
293.a. Ohio State University
294.a. Texas Tech University
295.a. University of Hawaii
296.a. University of South Florida
297.b. University of Arkansas
298.a. University of Wisconsin
299.a. University of Notre Dame

300. b. University of Wisconsin
301. c. Michael Phelps
302. b. Gabby Douglas
303. c. Jim Hines
304. b. Carl Lewis
305. b. Wilma Rudolph
306. a. Munich 1972
307. a. Michael Phelps
308. a. Peggy Fleming
309. a. Frank Shorter
310. b. Snowboarding
311. a. Dick Fosbury
312. b. Ronda Rousey
313. c. Natalie Coughlin
314. b. Downhill
315. b. Athens, Greece
316. b. Berlin, Germany
317. a. 1900 Paris Olympics
318. b. 1980
319. b. Los Angeles, USA
320. b. The Munich massacre
321. b. Tokyo, Japan
322. b. 1924
323. a. Atlanta, USA
324. b. Tokyo, Japan
325. c. London, England
326. a. Rome, Italy
327. b. Barcelona 1992
328. b. Tommie Smith and John Carlos
329. b. 1980 Moscow
330. a. Sydney 2000
331. b. Ben Johnson
332. b. Tonya Harding
333. c. 1992 Barcelona
334. a. Soviet Union
335. b. Rio 2016
336. b. 1988 Seoul
337. c. Laurel Hubbard
338. a. Iran
339. b. 1968 Mexico City
340. b. 1980 Lake Placid
341. c. Laurel Hubbard
342. b. 1980 Moscow
343. a. 2000 Sydney
344. b. 1972 Munich
345. c. Sweden
346. a. 1920 Antwerp

347.b. Ibtihaj Muhammad
348.a. North Korea and South Korea
349.b. Rose Nathike Lokonyen
350.c. 1996 Atlanta (Referring to Kerri Strug's famous vault)
351.b. San Jose, California
352.b. Tab Ramos
353.c. 1994
354.b. Brandi Chastain
355.b. 2002
356.b. Landon Donovan
357.a. Columbus, Ohio
358.b. David Beckham
359.a. D.C. United
360.a. 1991
361.d. Belo Horizonte Miracle
362.b. 2007
363.a. Liverpool vs. AC Milan
364.c. Belo Horizonte
365.b. England
366.a. The Maracanazo
367.a. France vs. Italy
368.a. 1999
369.a. Argentina vs. Uruguay
370.a. Chile
371.a. Greece
372.c. Bayern Munich
373.a. France
374.a. Scotland
375.c. Pelé
376.c. Lionel Messi
377.b. Miroslav Klose
378.b. Marta
379.a. David Beckham
380.b. Diego Maradona
381.a. Cristiano Ronaldo
382.a. Johan Cruyff
383.c. Teddy Sheringham
384.a. Diego Maradona
385.c. Zinedine Zidane
386.a. George Weah
387.d. Sadio Mané
388.b. Brazil

389.a. River Plate and Boca Juniors
390.c. St. Pauli
391.b. South America
392.b. Florence, Italy
393.b. Cameroon
394.a. 1914
395.c. Hidetoshi Nakata
396.c. Celtic and Rangers
397.b. Cameroon
398.c. Brazil
399.c. Uruguay
400.b. Racism

★ ★ ★ ★ ★

SHARE YOUR THOUGHTS!

Dear Reader,

As the author, I find your feedback invaluable. Your insights and opinions enhance my understanding of this book's impact and significantly influence my future work! Please consider leaving an honest review because your feedback guides other readers and helps us grow.

How to Leave a Review

Scan the QR code, which will take you to the review page.

Your voice matters. Lend it to the conversation and help shape future reads!

Thank you.

Printed in Great Britain
by Amazon